THE

by Mark Ravenhill

FOR AMATEUR PRODUCTION ENQUIRIES

UNITED KINGDOM AND WORLD
EXCLUDING NORTH AMERICA
licensing@concordtheatricals.co.uk
020-7054-7298

Each title is subject to availability from Concord Theatricals,
depending upon country of performance.

The moral right of Mark Ravenhill to be identified as author of this work has been asserted in accordance with Section 77 of the Copyright, Designs and Patents Act 1988.

USE OF COPYRIGHTED MUSIC

A licence issued by Concord Theatricals to perform this play does not include permission to use the incidental music specified in this publication. In the United Kingdom: Where the place of performance is already licensed by the PERFORMING RIGHT SOCIETY (PRS) a return of the music used must be made to them. If the place of performance is not so licensed then application should be made to PRS for Music (www.prsformusic.com). A separate and additional licence from PHONOGRAPHIC PERFORMANCE LTD (www.ppluk.com) may be needed whenever commercial recordings are used. Outside the United Kingdom: Please contact the appropriate music licensing authority in your territory for the rights to any incidental music.

USE OF COPYRIGHTED THIRD-PARTY MATERIALS

Licensees are solely responsible for obtaining formal written permission from copyright owners to use copyrighted third-party materials (e.g., artworks, logos) in the performance of this play and are strongly cautioned to do so. If no such permission is obtained by the licensee, then the licensee must use only original materials that the licensee owns and controls. Licensees are solely responsible and liable for clearances of all third-party copyrighted materials, and shall indemnify the copyright owners of the play(s) and their licensing agent, Concord Theatricals Ltd., against any costs, expenses, losses and liabilities arising from the use of such copyrighted third-party materials by licensees.

IMPORTANT BILLING AND CREDIT REQUIREMENTS

If you have obtained performance rights to this title, please refer to your licensing agreement for important billing and credit requirements.

THE CANE was first produced at Royal Court Theatre on 6th December 2019. The performance was directed by Vicky Featherstone, with design by Chloe Lamford, lighting design by Natasha Chivers, and sound design by David McSeveney. The cast was as follows:

ANNA . . . . Nicola Walker
MAUREEN. . . . . Maggie Steed
EDWARD. . . . . Alun Armstrong

CHARACTERS

ANNA
MAUREEN
EDWARD

TIME

December 2018

ONE

ANNA. What happened?

MAUREEN. The window broke.

ANNA. How did the window break?

MAUREEN. This is a temporary arrangement.

ANNA. Did someone break the window or?

MAUREEN. Until a glazier arrives.

ANNA. Who broke the window?

MAUREEN. It's very difficult at the weekend to find a glazier.

ANNA. Did someone

MAUREEN. I've been calling and calling but no reply

ANNA. Throw something through the window? Tell me. Mother.

MAUREEN. That's right yes someone threw something through the window.

ANNA. What did they throw?

MAUREEN. I was in the kitchen, heard the smash.

ANNA. What did they throw through the window?

MAUREEN. Lucky really that neither of us was in the room. It was a stone.

ANNA. Did you keep the stone?

MAUREEN. Actually more of a brick. A smallish

ANNA. Brick! Have you?

MAUREEN. Thrown away in the rubbish along with the glass.

ANNA. You should have kept the brick. The brick is evidence.

MAUREEN. Evidence?

ANNA. The police will want to see

MAUREEN. Oh no

ANNA. What was used to attack.

MAUREEN. Your father won't want to involve the police.

ANNA. When someone is throwing bricks through your window

MAUREEN. A child or children, a few children

ANNA. Did you see the children?

MAUREEN. Oh no.

ANNA. You didn't see the children?

MAUREEN. I was in the kitchen, he was in his study. He's got a report very important report that he's working on in his study.

ANNA. How do you know children threw the brick?

MAUREEN. I heard them.

ANNA. What did you hear?

MAUREEN. They laughed and they you know

ANNA. What?

MAUREEN. Called names.

ANNA. What names did they call?

MAUREEN. It doesn't matter.

ANNA. Insulting names?

MAUREEN. That was yesterday. It's all very quiet today.

ANNA. Were they insulting you or him? Who was the target of?

MAUREEN. You've picked a bad time. Could you maybe come back another day?

ANNA. I could find a glazier.

MAUREEN. No thank you.

ANNA. I'd like to help in some

MAUREEN. I've given him noise blocking headphones. Whatever they throw at us he can block out the noise and carry on in his study working on his report. I bought the headphones last week for his birthday.

ANNA. Is this a pattern?

MAUREEN. Did you forget that it was his birthday or?

ANNA. Was this an isolated incident?

MAUREEN. Not altogether no. This is really not a good time. I'm expecting the Head.

ANNA. The Headteacher's coming here?

MAUREEN. That's right.

ANNA. On a Sunday morning?

MAUREEN. That's right.

ANNA. Is it usual for the Head to conduct off-site meetings on a Sunday?

MAUREEN. Not usual no.

ANNA. The Head's coming here because it's pupils from the school who threw the brick through the window.

MAUREEN. The Head's coming here to finalise the leaving do on Friday. Your father's leaving do. You hadn't thought had you? That he's now leaving the school. Forty-five years. It will be the biggest send off that any teacher has ever had. No teacher is as loved. Friday will be full of song and praise.

ANNA. But the kids are throwing

MAUREEN. A few of the kids

ANNA. Bricks through the window. Why would they attack the most popular teacher in the school?

MAUREEN. Shouldn't you be looking after your family on a Sunday morning?

ANNA. I have an au pair.

MAUREEN. An au pair?

ANNA. I pay him very well.

MAUREEN. Why have you come?

ANNA. I suppose because I missed his birthday and

MAUREEN. You've missed his birthday for years, we've missed your birthday for years. So why?

ANNA. I wanted to catch up with you. Mother. Father. Only daughter.

MAUREEN. Well, now that you've caught up.

ANNA. Who patched the window?

MAUREEN. Me and him.

ANNA. You held the ladder?

MAUREEN. That's right.

ANNA. You held the ladder while he banged in the nails?

MAUREEN. That's it.

ANNA. Why did he never let me hold the ladder?

MAUREEN. Did you want to hold the ladder?

ANNA. Yes I did want to hold the ladder yes. I was always asking to hold the ladder. But he never let me hold the ladder. Why was that do you suppose?

MAUREEN. I suppose because when you lived here you were a child.

ANNA. I was a full-grown woman when I left.

MAUREEN. I never thought of you like that yes but I suppose you were a full-grown woman when you left.

ANNA. But still I never got to hold the ladder. Why?

MAUREEN. Maybe

ANNA. Yes

MAUREEN. He never trusted you to hold the ladder. It needs a steady hand otherwise the ladder wobbles

ANNA. I have a steady hand

MAUREEN. No you were volatile.

ANNA. I don't think I was

MAUREEN. Oh yes you were a very angry child. One time you tore this room apart.

ANNA. I don't remember that.

MAUREEN. Screaming and shouting, fuck this, fuck that, I'm going to kill him.

ANNA. I have absolutely no memory

MAUREEN. And you ripped the pictures from the wall, smashed the pots, chair into the mirror.

ANNA. I think if that happened I would have

MAUREEN. Is it any wonder then if he wouldn't let you hold the ladder? You have to trust the person holding the ladder because if you get to the top and they tug you could fall and they would break your neck.

ANNA. I would never have

MAUREEN. No?

ANNA. Have broken his neck no.

MAUREEN. Why I used to wonder is this small child so angry? Has anyone ever done anything to her that could possibly? And I thought no. It's – it must be – it's a chemical imbalance. It was impossible to love you. I suppose you've also forgotten the axe?

ANNA. The axe below the stairs?

MAUREEN. That's right yes the axe below the stairs.

ANNA. I remember the axe below the stairs.

MAUREEN. The day you got the axe from below the stairs and you were swinging the axe and screaming at him: I'm going to fucking cut your head off.

ANNA. No! That didn't.

MAUREEN. Oh yes chasing him. Axe swinging. Screaming.

ANNA. That certainly never – you are – this is a fairy story – you're –

MAUREEN. What are these marks on the wall? How do you explain these if they're not? Can you see the marks? Yes?

ANNA. Anyone else would have decorated every five years.

MAUREEN. This is where the axe went into the wall when you were aiming for your father's head. We've never had the sort of money to decorate. Au pairs. There'll be money when the endowment from the mortgage comes through, the pension then we'll finally. We'll be comfortable.

ANNA. You need both of you to.

MAUREEN. I hope you're not expecting to

ANNA. New wallpaper, new furniture, loft conversion.

MAUREEN. We're not planning to share

ANNA. I understand

MAUREEN. In case you were expecting a windfall.

ANNA. I want to see Daddy.

MAUREEN. He won't want to see you.

ANNA. Let him be the judge.

MAUREEN. He's working on a very important report and he mustn't –

ANNA. Dad! Hello Dad! It's me!

MAUREEN. The noise-defying headphones are very effective.

ANNA. Where's his study?

MAUREEN. Doesn't [matter].

ANNA. Where?

MAUREEN. Your room.

ANNA. Oh.

MAUREEN. Ten years ago we made a bonfire and we took out all your stuff out of your room and we put it on the bonfire and we burnt it all away.

ANNA. Why did you do that?

MAUREEN. I suppose we didn't want any memory of you. I suppose because as a child you were an angry violent little girl and as an adult –

ANNA. Fuck you.

MAUREEN. This is exactly what I

ANNA. You cunt you bitch fuck.

MAUREEN.   Exactly exactly. A few children throwing stones? Broken window. You see it's nothing compared to. He suggested the bonfire because he said you'd taken such a different path and you weren't coming back and we didn't want anything more to do with you.

ANNA. Different path.

MAUREEN. When you joined the opposition.

ANNA. Academy schools are not the / opposition.

MAUREEN. Oh they are.

ANNA. I joined the academy schools movement because it's the best model to turn around failing schools.

MAUREEN. Marketisation.

ANNA. To save young people who have been failed by their schools.

MAUREEN. Profits from a human right.

ANNA. In a challenging economic and social environment.

MAUREEN. Grab the money.

ANNA. To connect young people to the world of work, to prepare them for employment, to link the school to business, to the real world. There's no better offer that we can make to the next generation. If we don't give them everything they need to compete in the marketplace then we've failed them haven't we?

MAUREEN. It's time you were gone. The Head will be here any minute. It would be better.

> *(Noises off.)*

ANNA. What's that?

MAUREEN. The children. They must be back again. They bang and they shout. I'm used to it.

ANNA. They shouldn't be allowed to do it.

MAUREEN. We can still go about our usual routine.

ANNA. If you're not going to call the police then I'll deal with them myself.

MAUREEN. How will you deal with them yourself?

ANNA. I'll talk to them, explain that this is unacceptable behaviour, that any dispute will be settled by the school and failing that by the police.

MAUREEN. Try. Open the door. Try.

ANNA. I will.

MAUREEN. You'll get what's coming to you.

ANNA. What does that mean? Get what's coming to you?

MAUREEN. It means that when you step outside the door they will spit at you, they will jostle, call names and they will throw things such as bottles, bricks and dog shit.

ANNA. They do this to you?

MAUREEN. I've stopped going through the door.

ANNA. How long have you stopped going through the door?

MAUREEN. Six days.

ANNA. You've both been trapped in the house for six days?

MAUREEN. It's been quite useful really because it's allowed him to focus on his report and it's allowed me to focus on looking after him while he finishes his report.

ANNA. I don't think the Head is

MAUREEN. He'll make it through

ANNA. He's not going to come calling when there's a mob outside the front door.

MAUREEN. He'll come. He's a very loyal. Entirely loyal man. He wants to make sure that Daddy has a wonderful send off on Friday.

ANNA. It's never best practice to hold an off-site meeting outside of working hours.

MAUREEN. Please no don't bring that bullshit in here. It stinks the place out.

ANNA. Why have the children turned against him?

MAUREEN. Children are like that.

ANNA. Why now when he's just about to retire are they mobbing the house? Listen to them. There has to be a reason.

MAUREEN. What was the reason for your anger?

ANNA. What's he done to them?

MAUREEN. He's done nothing to them but offer excellent teaching and pastoral care.

ANNA. Then why?

MAUREEN. Go away.

ANNA. Why?

MAUREEN. They claim it's

ANNA. Yes?

MAUREEN. Because of the cane.

ANNA. The cane?

MAUREEN. Go away.

ANNA. The cane.

MAUREEN. Because of all the boys that he caned.

ANNA. Where did he cane boys?

MAUREEN. Well at the school of course. Where else would you cane boys?

ANNA. When?

MAUREEN. When it was legal to cane boys.

ANNA. That was

MAUREEN. Over thirty years ago. The Head – not this Head, a much older – didn't want it as part of his duties so he made it the duty of the deputy to cane the boys. You don't remember. You were a child.

ANNA. That explains. I was teased.

MAUREEN. Who?

ANNA. "Your daddy is at the big school and in the big school you can hear the screams all day long because there's a cellar where he chains children to the wall and he flogs them until they bleed."

MAUREEN. You didn't tell us that.

ANNA. Why should I have told you that?

MAUREEN. So that we could correct you. Your misapprehension. Did you believe the other children when they told you?

ANNA. I suppose I did believe them for a while yes.

MAUREEN. It was never anything like a cellar or

ANNA. Of course not

MAUREEN. It was a widely accepted practice

ANNA. I understood later but for a few years I did think

MAUREEN. What a foolish gullible silly little girl you were.

ANNA. He's never beaten any of these children now?

MAUREEN. Of course he hasn't

ANNA. Then why are these children?

MAUREEN. Because they're snowflakes. These children now can hunt out anybody's grievance and claim it as their own. They can't stand that the past wasn't just the same as today. If something was done differently in the past they bawl and they whine, kick and spit and attack.

ANNA. Young people today are much more aware

MAUREEN. You've got the modern tone of voice.

ANNA. Of issues relating to coercion, personal space, violence.

MAUREEN. They want to be offended.

ANNA. Why now? Something after thirty years must have.

MAUREEN. With his retirement – there's been a group organising his celebration – students – and they've been given access to the school records to put together a celebration of all Daddy's achievements at the school.

ANNA. And in the records they found evidence of his history of caning.

MAUREEN. I suppose they must have done. And the word spread around the school in a few hours until every child – all a thousand of them – was in a state of outrage.

ANNA. It must be very distressing for a young person to discover

MAUREEN. Only if they want to be

ANNA. that a man who is teaching you every day was in fact a beater of children. Has the school offered counselling?

MAUREEN. I don't think so.

ANNA. Best practice would be to offer any young person affected

MAUREEN. It would only encourage them

ANNA. A safe space to discuss any feelings that arise as

MAUREEN. To indulge themselves further in their introspection and self pity.

ANNA. Has he offered an apology?

MAUREEN. Has who offered an apology?

ANNA. Has Dad offered an apology?

MAUREEN. Why should he apologise?

ANNA. In a situation like this tensions can often be dispersed by a simple apology.

MAUREEN. Oh no.

ANNA. Stand before the school, acknowledge that in the past mistakes were made, recognise the mistakes, that the mistakes have been learnt from and that they won't be made in the future and ask forgiveness and then move forward to his leaving do on Friday.

MAUREEN. That would hardly be

ANNA. How many kids have turned up outside the house for the last six days?

MAUREEN. The numbers vary.

ANNA. How many on average?

MAUREEN. On average I would say late afternoon after school there are about a hundred children.

ANNA. A hundred!

MAUREEN. Which means there are another nine hundred or so who don't

ANNA. A hundred is more than enough to stop Friday happening.

MAUREEN. Which is why I've invited the Head here today. I want his assurance that the staff will lend their full support to protect everyone attending the farewell and to prevent any disruption or physical attack.

ANNA. If he just apologises.

MAUREEN. If you leave now

ANNA. I understand how to put together a form of words

MAUREEN. Go before the numbers build.

ANNA. That will operate as an apology without recognising any legal

MAUREEN. Leave it any longer and there'll be too many

ANNA. I can write it for him

MAUREEN. Once the crowd builds they become unruly

ANNA. Or write it with him

MAUREEN. Once they reach a critical mass they will attack on sight

ANNA. Coach him on the delivery

MAUREEN. Get out now go go why are you still here? Go.

ANNA. I'm very confident that all this would go away, that Friday would still be possible if only an apology were made.

MAUREEN. That's not something he would ever do.

ANNA. How can you be so sure?

MAUREEN. I know him, I understand him. You passed through our lives without ever understanding him at all.

ANNA. I'm going to ask him myself.

MAUREEN. Go on then. Up the stairs. Up the stairs, into his study. There's no point in calling him, no point in knocking. With the headphones on he won't hear a thing. You'll have to walk straight in, stand before him. Then you'll see how much he hates you.

ANNA. He doesn't hate me.

MAUREEN. I'm the one who says to him: Yes, she seems something swapped by an evil fairy for the baby we should have had.

ANNA. Hah!

MAUREEN. But she's ours. We must have made her, played our part to make her the person she is

ANNA. I think actually I made myself.

MAUREEN. So we should try to find a way to connect with her.

ANNA. I decided very early on that I would make myself.

MAUREEN. And now that there are grandchildren, we're grandparents, I think we should play a part in their lives.

ANNA. You said that?

MAUREEN. I've said that many, many times.

ANNA. And what's he said?

MAUREEN. He's said that he has his principles and as you've betrayed his principles that he will never have anything to do with you. And I respect him for that. If those are his principles then I have to be loyal to him. That's really the only way to make any sense of life. If I start to wonder about that it quickly leads to depression and then I'm completely useless. I become immobile. His principles are fixed and sometimes harsh but they make sense. You won't change his mind, you won't soften him. So really the kindest thing to do, the kindest to yourself is to leave and go back to your children and your au pair before the mob out there starts to attack. I should never have opened the door. If I'd known it was you, I would have let the bell ring and ring. It was only because I thought you were the Head that I opened the door at all.

ANNA. Thank you for opening the door.

*(Enter **EDWARD**.)*

EDWARD. Do you see that? One hundred and eighteen of them. It's a record. And so early in the morning. But then Sunday what else are they going to do? What better to do on a Sunday morning than to come round here and mob our house? Has the Head arrived? He's a terrible time keeper. We go on and on at the kids about time keeping but the Head's late for everything. The assembly hall is full and he's still scoffing his granola. He'll get here sooner or later. "Sorry, sorry, sorry." By the time he gets here, I'll have finished my report. One last, very straightforward section to complete and it can go off tomorrow. I can join you for your discussion about Friday. Why are you here?

ANNA. I missed your birthday.

EDWARD. And we missed yours. It's a family tradition.

ANNA. I said to your grandchildren that I'd missed your birthday and they said that they wanted to make you a card.

EDWARD. Well that's good.

ANNA. Art isn't their strength but still – as they made the card I felt I ought to – would you like to see the card?

EDWARD. Why not?

ANNA. Some of the stars fell off but it's still –

EDWARD. Well, look at that. See what they've done.

MAUREEN. Very nice.

EDWARD. Yes isn't it? That's very nice.

MAUREEN. Very nice.

ANNA. I didn't expect

EDWARD. Please say thank you to the children from both of us.

ANNA. To find.

EDWARD. And thank you for coming all this way.

ANNA. I had no idea

EDWARD. Ah well.

ANNA. That you were under siege.

EDWARD. These things happen. Schools are volatile communities. Things blow up and then they blow away again.

ANNA. If there's more of them than ever.

EDWARD. On Friday everything will be forgotten.

ANNA. If you were to offer an apology.

EDWARD. You think?

ANNA. "I was working at the time within an accepted practice but with hindsight I regret my actions and ask the school community to forgive" –

EDWARD. Ha!

ANNA. You don't feel any regret?

EDWARD. Goodbye.

ANNA. All the caned children?

EDWARD. Do we have any space on the pin board?

MAUREEN. It's full.

EDWARD. We don't seem to have anywhere to put this card. I had so many birthday cards – staff, students, old friends – it really is hard to find anywhere

ANNA. Give me the card.

EDWARD. But the children

ANNA. I'll tell them that you loved the card.

MAUREEN. Say goodbye to Daddy: he's off upstairs to finish his report.

EDWARD. Goodbye. Safe drive.

ANNA. Is your report a response to the inspectors?

EDWARD. That's right.

ANNA. The inspectors' findings that your school is –?

MAUREEN. Stop that now.

ANNA. The inspectors were very damning of your school. The inspectors found poor management, weak discipline, inadequate implementation of pupil voice, terrible results.

MAUREEN. That's not right.

ANNA. And the inspectors have recommended that the school be classified as a failing school. Isn't that right?

MAUREEN. She says it to upset you.

ANNA. Didn't he tell you Mum about the inspectors?

MAUREEN. I didn't ask.

ANNA. He didn't tell you that the inspectors have failed the school?

EDWARD. School inspections are by and large a political tool.

ANNA. It was a carefully chosen team from the worlds of business and education.

EDWARD. Weighted towards forcing us into an academy.

MAUREEN. They'll turn the school over to the academy?

EDWARD. No.

MAUREEN. You mustn't let the academy

EDWARD. The report I'm writing now refutes every single criticism.

ANNA. You can't deny

MAUREEN. How do you know

ANNA. The results are disastrous.

MAUREEN. What the inspectors wrote?

ANNA. The school is failing its students.

MAUREEN. Have you read the inspectors' report?

ANNA. I have yes read the inspectors' report.

MAUREEN. How have you read the inspectors' report?

ANNA. A friend

EDWARD. It's a draft

ANNA. Passed the report onto me and I read it.

MAUREEN. What friend?

ANNA. When you're in the same business.

MAUREEN. Don't call it that.

ANNA. When you're in the same field information is shared.

MAUREEN. Disastrous results! That's

EDWARD. It's a different school. It's not the same school as it was even ten years ago. Do you know how many languages are now spoken at the school? English is for many a second, third, fourth language. Some of the kids arrive from war zones. Civil wars in which they have often themselves fought. Kids in the classroom were only the week before facing drones and gas. And in those circumstances

ANNA. You're writing this in your report?

EDWARD. They're not comparing like for like.

ANNA. It's relevant background but only if you frame

EDWARD. The inspectors have to understand the conditions under which we work.

ANNA. But you need to frame – like is actually compared for like so –

(Noises off.)

EDWARD. Little bastards! Bugger off you little bastards! Go on! Hop it! It's not the refugees who cause the trouble. They keep their heads down. It's the fat, white, complacent – I told you to fuck off!

MAUREEN. Don't.

EDWARD. I've a good mind to

MAUREEN. Ignore them.

EDWARD. go out there and give them a piece of my mind.

ANNA. When you respond to an inspectors' report – I've read hundreds of reports, hundreds of responses – So many responses fail to engage with the language and the frame that the inspectors utilise. I can help you

EDWARD. I'm almost done.

ANNA. I can translate your response into the language spoken by the inspectors.

MAUREEN. He doesn't want to speak their language.

ANNA. He wants to challenge the failed school status. Yes, a lot of their language is bullshit. But if it takes a bit of bullshit to reply then

EDWARD. Alright yes.

ANNA. Yes?

EDWARD. Help me with my report.

MAUREEN. But.

EDWARD. Some of what they've written doesn't make sense to any normal human being. She's not a normal human being.

ANNA. Thank you.

EDWARD. She speaks jargon. That's very useful. I'll get the laptop. You deal with the Head while me and her. We'll sort out the inspectors.

(Exit **EDWARD**.*)*

MAUREEN. Why is the Head so late?

ANNA. I really don't think you should expect the Head to come. If the governors weren't mindful before about off-site meetings. Under the current circumstances, they'll be sure to prevent all off-site meetings. Any meetings with Dad will happen on site and with a member of the governors present. It's the way things have to be done under the current circumstances. When a school is failing it's vital to be mindful of best practice. Transparency

MAUREEN. Transparency!

ANNA. Is important.

MAUREEN. Were you transparent with the father of your children?

ANNA. I tried to

MAUREEN. Is that why he didn't hang around for long? It's actually very childish this need to know everything. We're together, me and him – forty-seven years – because we respect each other: little secrets, little lies. He has his. Fine. I have mine. An adult is a person who understands that some things can never be known.

ANNA. Like the cane?

MAUREEN. Yes like the cane.

ANNA. You never talked about the cane?

MAUREEN. He came home one day and said: I've been offered Deputy Head and I said: that's marvellous. And I knew what that meant. We both knew what it meant. The Deputy Head caned the naughty boys. That was part of the job.

ANNA. Didn't you ever want to ask him:

MAUREEN. No

ANNA. "Have you caned your first boy yet?"

MAUREEN. No.

ANNA. "How many boys have you caned? What does it feel like to cane a boy? Is it upsetting?"

MAUREEN. These are all very modern

ANNA. And when the legislation changed did you say: "Well isn't this good? You don't have to cane boys any more?"

MAUREEN. I didn't mention it before, I didn't mention it during, I didn't mention it after.

ANNA. You were ashamed

MAUREEN. It wasn't

ANNA. Of the brutality.

MAUREEN. Do you tell your children about the redundancies you make? Do you go home and report every case of intimidation of staff in your academy schools?

ANNA. My children

MAUREEN. Of the institutional culture of management bullying in the pursuit of profit?

ANNA. When there are restrictive practices, complacency

MAUREEN. Then you bully them away?

ANNA. A school isn't there for the teachers. It's for the students. A safe environment in which they can prepare for the world of work. That's what parents and students want and that's what we deliver.

MAUREEN. Why did you come today?

ANNA. My children were very insistent that I delivered their grandfather's birthday card.

MAUREEN. Did you come maybe because you'd read the inspectors' report?

ANNA. That wasn't

MAUREEN. And you thought that if your academy was going to make a grab for the school to become part of its portfolio

ANNA. That's a very paranoid reading.

MAUREEN. Do you want to take over Daddy's school?

ANNA. An offer to help with his response to the inspectors' report is hardly indicative.

MAUREEN. Promise me you won't try to take over Daddy's school.

ANNA. It's not his school.

MAUREEN. If I had to guess I would say no. He didn't want to cane. He's not naturally. He's actually a very kind man. His dad wasn't. His dad was a cruel man who would belt him if he stepped out of line. When you smashed up this room, when you came at him with the axe what did Daddy do? You don't remember? He talked to you calmly, waited until your rage passed. He didn't cane the boys because he was cruel but because that's what the school demanded of him. So yes I should imagine yes that caused him yes shame, regret, grief, yes I would say all of those things. But he did what the school expected. His school. So I want you to promise

*(Enter **EDWARD**.)*

EDWARD. A hundred and forty-seven of them now. I thought that the numbers might be less today.

MAUREEN. What's their mood?

EDWARD. I should say bloody.

MAUREEN. Bloody?

EDWARD. As in ready to kill.

ANNA. I would have thought the police

EDWARD. Oh no.

ANNA. Why don't the police provide

EDWARD. It's a school matter.

ANNA. You're not at school now.

EDWARD. The police have always been a very last resort.

ANNA. A hundred and forty-seven children in a bloody mood.

EDWARD. There are some adults now.

ANNA. Maybe there are some of your former

EDWARD. Yes?

ANNA. Former

EDWARD. Were you going to say victims?

ANNA. I wouldn't

EDWARD. They do use that word. That's a word they use on their placards and graffiti 'victims'

MAUREEN. It's a silly word.

EDWARD. And lord help us 'survivors'. Were you going to use the word survivors?

ANNA. Neither of those words.

EDWARD. What word were you then going to use?

ANNA. Would you recognise one of the boys who you once caned?

EDWARD. I don't think so. They grow old, get bald, get fat and so no I don't think I would recognise no.

MAUREEN. If you're going to help him with his report don't you think you better get on with the job?

ANNA. Yes I suppose we better had.

MAUREEN. I'm not sure that there's any point you starting the work down here not when the Head's just about to arrive.

EDWARD. No?

MAUREEN. It would be better for you both to go into your study and start the work there.

ANNA. I'd rather work down here.

MAUREEN. Would you?

ANNA. Yes I would.

MAUREEN. Why's that?

ANNA. I don't want to work in a room from which all my stuff was taken and burnt.

EDWARD. We'll work here.

MAUREEN. When the Head

ANNA. If the Head comes, we'll move.

MAUREEN. Alright. It's best not to have tea or coffee near a laptop. A cup of tea or coffee near a laptop can easily be spilled in my experience. Even a few drops of tea or coffee spilled on a laptop and the laptop dies and all the work can be lost. That's my experience of a laptop.

EDWARD. Would you like a pen and a piece of paper?

ANNA. I won't need them.

EDWARD. If you're going to make notes as you go along.

ANNA. There's a function which allows you to make notes directly on to the document.

EDWARD. Is there really?

ANNA. Like this.

EDWARD. Well, look at that. Why didn't I know about that before?

MAUREEN. Do you think I should scrub up for the Head? War paint and maybe a skirt? I think that gays like a bit of glamour in a woman. I suppose because it reminds them of their mothers. Well, lipstick certainly wouldn't do any harm. This is the mirror that we bought thirty-two years ago. We bought the mirror to replace the mirror that you smashed during your rage. You remember the mirror that she smashed during her rage?

EDWARD. I'm sorry I can only focus on

MAUREEN. And your hand bled when you picked up the pieces.

EDWARD. I don't remember that.

MAUREEN. Gushing from the wound.

EDWARD. I have no memory at all.

MAUREEN. When she destroyed this room.

EDWARD. Did she? Did you?

MAUREEN. You must remember the way she swung the axe. Look here are the marks on the wall.

EDWARD. Ha! Oh yes I remember that. A grown man being chased around the room by a little girl with an axe. Ha!

MAUREEN. You can laugh about it now.

EDWARD. Yes I can laugh about it now. If I think about it at all.

ANNA. I'm striking a line through the irrelevant sections.

MAUREEN. Don't you think it's suspicious?

EDWARD. What's that?

MAUREEN. Suspicious that all this is happening now.

EDWARD. That all what's happening now?

MAUREEN. That these children are turning against you now? That at the moment when you're leading the fight back against the academy

EDWARD. What are you suggesting?

MAUREEN. I suppose what I'm suggesting is that someone

EDWARD. Who?

MAUREEN. Has sought to undermine you by leaking

EDWARD. Who would do that?

MAUREEN. Knowing that the children would become inflamed and disrupt your work.

EDWARD. You think that someone within the school?

MAUREEN. Possibly yes within the school

EDWARD. I don't think so

MAUREEN. Maybe in collusion with someone from the academy.

EDWARD. We are united in our opposition to the academy.

MAUREEN. She was aware of your history of caning.

EDWARD. Were you?

ANNA. Yes I was.

MAUREEN. Don't you think it's possible that she has in some way colluded

EDWARD. Her? No! I don't think she would – Have you?

ANNA. No!

EDWARD. Only one item exists as a record of my part in the school's history of caning.

MAUREEN. One item?

EDWARD. Just one.

MAUREEN. Which one?

EDWARD. A ledger. The black book in which successive Deputies recorded date, name of boy, cause of caning, parents' permission, signature of staff member giving the cane, number of strokes given according to the school guidelines, countersigned by the Head.

MAUREEN. These children must have got hold of the ledger.

EDWARD. No. It's not possible that any child recently could have seen the ledger.

MAUREEN. Why's that?

EDWARD. Because I removed the ledger from the school archive some time ago.

ANNA. You tampered with the archive?

EDWARD. It was a forgotten item, lost in a box file, gathering dust at the back of a cupboard.

ANNA. That's not a matter of best practice

EDWARD. No I don't suppose

ANNA. If the inspectors were aware that you were removing school records.

EDWARD. When I became aware several months ago that there was to be a celebration for my retirement

ANNA. Where did the ledger?

EDWARD. And that the celebration would take the form of a history of my time at the school

ANNA. Is the ledger still on site or?

EDWARD. I did think: ah they'll be looking through the archives, research all my achievements at the school and then I remembered: yes the ledger, my signature beside several hundred canings.

ANNA. You felt guilt?

EDWARD. Maybe something like guilt I suppose yes.

MAUREEN. You have no reason to

EDWARD. But mostly I thought: well this will come as a shock to the little buggers. This will seem like something from the past, cruel like sending children up chimneys. And I did have some idea that yes this might result in a movement against me.

ANNA. Where's the ledger now?

EDWARD. Now the ledger is. I slipped it in my coat pocket and I brought it home with me.

ANNA. It's here?

EDWARD. That's right I've kept it here for the last few months.

ANNA. In your study?

EDWARD. No here you see in the drawer with the odds and sods. Everybody's handwriting was very neat back then. No computers so I suppose. With a fountain pen you see? The first entry is just one week after the comprehensive school opened. Somebody must have ordered new stationery. The first Deputy Head who signed had taught at the school when it was a single-sex grammar. Military man. Been at Dunkirk. And here you see is where my hand takes over. I couldn't write like that now. Our hands have all become somehow lazier now haven't they? A couple of changes of Head Teacher you'll notice during my time. And here the last entry actually several months before the legislation ended caning. It was still legally possible to cane a boy but we could see which way the wind was blowing so... When you look at the names now they all look very English don't they? All of them white boys. Nowadays the school community is much more diverse.

MAUREEN. I think it would have been better to destroy

EDWARD. Destroy?

MAUREEN. If you thought that this had the potential to turn them against you then yes we could have built a bonfire

EDWARD. I suppose

MAUREEN. Put it on the bonfire and burnt it away.

EDWARD. We could have done that yes.

MAUREEN. If we could build a bonfire now

EDWARD. I don't think now

MAUREEN. But with the mob outside that would only draw attention

EDWARD. That's right

ANNA. It's actually better – removing and destroying would be – removing is very bad practice but still – it's good that you have this. If we're going to successfully manage the disclosure of your history of caning this will be a useful document. Evidence that you weren't individually culpable.

MAUREEN. Nobody thinks that he's –

ANNA. You never caned without parental permission?

EDWARD. That's the way it worked. A phone call to the father or mother to give the go ahead.

ANNA. And if the parents withheld permission?

EDWARD. They very rarely did. I can recall I think only two or three instances in which parental permission was refused.

ANNA. Hundreds of parents allowed

EDWARD. As you can see.

MAUREEN. That's how it was. There was respect. Teachers were respected. If the Deputy Head recommended a course of action, the parent deferred. The school knew what was best for the child.

ANNA. Each of the Heads has counter signed. Clear evidence of a culture of caning. Institutionalised violence. We can make a case that the institution and not the individual

EDWARD. I suppose we can. Yes. I feel –

ANNA. Yes?

EDWARD. I feel somewhat – ha – diminished.

ANNA. Diminished?

EDWARD. Yes diminished to discover that all along I was not an individual but an institution.

ANNA. That's what will save you.

EDWARD. Then so be it.

ANNA. I'll keep this safe.

MAUREEN. With this, they can contact any boy who was ever caned, enlist him to their cause. Wouldn't it be better?

ANNA. A bonfire isn't always the best solution in my experience.

EDWARD. Shall we continue with the report? Once the report's done and the crowd has calmed down we can look forward to Friday. Where's the Head do you think?

MAUREEN. I should say he's on his way.

EDWARD. Don't you think it would be best to have cake and coffee ready for the Head when he arrives?

MAUREEN. I suppose it would.

EDWARD. Maybe if you get the cake and the coffee ready while we work on the report?

MAUREEN. I'll do that if you like.

EDWARD. Yes I'd like that very much.

MAUREEN. Alright.

        (Exit **MAUREEN**.*)*

EDWARD. Tell me honestly – you can be honest with me – what you think of my report.

ANNA. I should say

EDWARD. I haven't I confess kept up with all the latest words.

ANNA. It's very passionate.

EDWARD. Do you think so?

ANNA. You express yourself with great passion, your love of the school, of its history, the children, you write about them with passion.

EDWARD. I don't suppose the inspectors

ANNA. The inspectors have their own passion which they express in a different way. The desire to drive up standards in every school is a great passion in itself.

EDWARD. Which is also your passion?

ANNA. That's right, it's also my passion.

EDWARD. Funny how you get used to things.

ANNA. Such as?

EDWARD. I stopped seeing those axe marks in the wall years ago. But once they're pointed out to you they're actually quite deep aren't they?

ANNA. If you'd ever wallpapered.

EDWARD. Yes that would have done the trick. I spent all my time at the school, let this place go to rack and ruin. After Friday there's going to be plenty of time. An eternity. I'll wallpaper this and there'll be no reminder that the axe was ever swung.

ANNA. I can't explain

EDWARD. I'm not asking you to

ANNA. Why I did that. Maybe it was a chemical.

EDWARD. I suppose it's a very normal feeling isn't it?

ANNA. What feeling?

EDWARD. I want to murder Daddy. I was never bothered about it, not even when you came towards me with the axe but your mum's an old worrier so I suppose...

ANNA. You'll wallpaper it yourself?

EDWARD. I should think so

ANNA. You won't

EDWARD. Oh no.

ANNA. Get a man in?

EDWARD. I'll have to do something to fill up all that time won't I?

ANNA. If you need someone to hold the ladder.

EDWARD. She always holds the ladder.

ANNA. You know that you can always ask me to hold the ladder. Whose idea was it to burn all my stuff?

EDWARD. You hadn't been here for years.

ANNA. Who actually lit the bonfire? Did you light the bonfire or did she?

EDWARD. That was a long time ago. I suppose – man of the house – I lit the bonfire.

ANNA. You remember that?

EDWARD. Not exactly but it's the sort of thing the man does isn't it? The woman clears out the room while the man chops the wood and then he lights the flame. At least, that's the way it is for us. The older generation.

ANNA. We can make a good case

EDWARD. You think so?

ANNA. If we take the passion here and put in a form of words which the inspectors recognise as

EDWARD. Good.

ANNA. We can make a robust case for the school to be given time to put in place an effective action plan.

EDWARD. What's pupil voice?

ANNA. Pupil voice is

EDWARD. It's popped up a lot the last few years but I've never fully understood

ANNA. Every school is expected to have a working model for pupil voice.

EDWARD. Is it the same as school council?

ANNA. It might include a school council yes but it's a more holistic approach to

EDWARD. It's listening to the kids.

ANNA. In essence yes it's listening to the kids.

EDWARD. We listen to the kids.

ANNA. Are you sure? The inspectors are very critical

EDWARD. We're very good at listening to the kids.

ANNA. This wouldn't have happened.

EDWARD. This?

ANNA. The window wouldn't be boarded up if the school had already implemented a best practice model of pupil voice.

EDWARD. I don't always follow what you're saying.

(Enter **MAUREEN**.)

MAUREEN. The coffee's Fairtrade and the tarts are of Portuguese origin. I think it's best if you put away the laptop now. I want to use the table for the coffee and a laptop and coffee should never be on the same table. Why don't you take the laptop up to the study so that I can deal with the Head?

ANNA. What's planned for Friday?

MAUREEN. I'm not altogether sure.

ANNA. Will the whole school?

MAUREEN. I should imagine yes the school and former staff and students yes I imagine.

EDWARD. She imagines.

MAUREEN. That's the sort of send off I imagine you'd give to a man who's dedicated forty-five years of his life to a school.

EDWARD. She knows

MAUREEN. I know

EDWARD. Exactly what they've got planned for Friday.

MAUREEN. Do I?

EDWARD. Yes you do.

MAUREEN. How would I possibly know that?

EDWARD. Because you've been a part – a very active part – of the group that's organising

MAUREEN. Oh really? Really?

EDWARD. The group's been meeting here while I

MAUREEN. You seem to know an awful lot

EDWARD. Yes I do.

MAUREEN. How do you know so much?

EDWARD. Because I have spies.

MAUREEN. Spies! Ha! Well, if I'd known there were spies.

ANNA. Listen I think you should be prepared

EDWARD. Yes?

ANNA. If the Head does come today to this off-site meeting

MAUREEN. He's coming

ANNA. I think you should be prepared to discuss with the Head the possibility of a postponement

MAUREEN. Oh no.

ANNA. Of Friday's event. I think it would be wise to postpone.

MAUREEN. We can't give in.

ANNA. When the school is under special scrutiny from the inspectors it would be reckless

MAUREEN. Reckless!

ANNA. To risk an event which could be at best chaotic and could become a violent

MAUREEN. We'll stop that happening.

ANNA. What difference would it make to wait for a few months

MAUREEN. Why should a man who has given up his life?

ANNA. Until you know where you stand with the inspectors, until you've adequately dealt with the disclosure of the history of caning? You understand don't you that Friday is not a good time when

EDWARD. I see that yes.

ANNA. Once you're through the woods and out into the fresh air, when you're in a better place, when the school's – yes?

EDWARD. Yes that makes a great deal of sense. Only

ANNA. Yes?

EDWARD. I've been looking forward to Friday.

MAUREEN. We've all been looking forward to Friday.

EDWARD. I very much want Friday to go ahead.

ANNA. But in the current circumstances.

EDWARD. I think we should resolve to make Friday happen.

ANNA. No!

EDWARD. I need – my last day – other teachers chop and change – maybe I should have chopped and changed – but I never chopped and changed – I've stayed with the same school – I've moved upwards, backwards, sideways – I've spent forty-five years at the same school and now I want – I suppose I must be a very vain man but I want

ANNA. Yes?

EDWARD. To be thanked, to be praised.

ANNA. In time

EDWARD. To stand on the stage and to see them all below and looking up at me and to feel their gratitude. My spies tell me that they've planned for Friday a sort of play is that right?

MAUREEN. How would I know?

EDWARD. She knows! A pageant of my time at the school. The young man arriving with a guitar and a head full of fresh ideas. Learning to master the classroom.

EDWARD. Moving towards the centre of the school community. Fundraising for the minibus, driving the minibus, pranging the minibus. Falling out with one Head, falling in with the next. Upwards: the heights of department head, deputy of the school. Working out when to use the carrot, when to use the – the metaphorical stick.

MAUREEN. There is a pageant planned for Friday.

EDWARD. I knew it!

MAUREEN. Little scenes, readings, songs.

EDWARD. Who'll play me?

MAUREEN. Ah.

EDWARD. Which of the little buggers will take my part?

MAUREEN. These are secrets.

EDWARD. I think I can be allowed to know a few

ANNA. If we're going to work upstairs – are you coming upstairs?

EDWARD. You won't recognise the room.

ANNA. I'm curious to see

EDWARD. Every last fixture and fitting replaced.

MAUREEN. It won't be just one of them playing you.

EDWARD. Really?

MAUREEN. There will be a whole series

EDWARD. Ha!

MAUREEN. Playing you through the decades. Some in the scenes, some in the songs

EDWARD. Wonderful!

MAUREEN. You will be played by several boys and also by a couple of girls.

EDWARD. Girls!

MAUREEN. All the colours, genders so that everything is

EDWARD. Inclusive

MAUREEN. Inclusive exactly yes. They're a very charming bunch. I like them.

ANNA. Shall I take this upstairs and start the work by myself?

EDWARD. They've been here?

MAUREEN. I've said enough.

EDWARD. The kids performing the pageant have been here?

MAUREEN. I've said more than enough. Both of you go upstairs to your study and work on the report.

EDWARD. I want to know

MAUREEN. Well then. Yes actually the kids did come here.

EDWARD. Aha!

MAUREEN. For their costumes.

EDWARD. Costumes?

MAUREEN. They want to wear your clothes.

EDWARD. These old

MAUREEN. Not your clothes now but your clothes then. The children are planning in the performance to wear your actual clothes throughout the decades.

EDWARD. The clothes that I

MAUREEN. That every few years you put in the bin bags and then I hold the ladder each time you put a new bundle in the attic, yes.

EDWARD. You went up into the attic and brought down the clothes?

MAUREEN. Oh no I held the ladder.

EDWARD. So who went into the attic?

MAUREEN. Several of the children.

EDWARD. You held the ladder while

MAUREEN. Several of the children went into the attic and brought down the clothes.

ANNA. We should focus our energies on the section on pupil voice.

EDWARD. Did you think that was a wise thing to do?

MAUREEN. I didn't think if

EDWARD. Didn't you think it might be unwise to allow kids to go marauding through the attic?

MAUREEN. They didn't maraud. I would have heard them if they marauded.

EDWARD. What then?

MAUREEN. They went directly to the bags and brought them down.

EDWARD. How could they have gone directly to the bags when only I

ANNA. Can we continue our work?

EDWARD. When only I know where the bags are. When only I know where anything is in the attic. The attic is organised according to my system. And now I find that you

MAUREEN. I'm sorry if I'd known

EDWARD. Allow children

MAUREEN. It was so important.

EDWARD. Together for forty-seven years I think you know how important

MAUREEN. I'm sorry I'm sorry I'm sorry

EDWARD. I can only imagine the destruction

MAUREEN. Destruction

EDWARD. Destruction that they have wreaked in my attic.

ANNA. The attic isn't the important

EDWARD. Yes it is yes the attic is very the most important yes.

ANNA. Why is the attic important?

EDWARD. What are the names of the kids who went into the attic?

MAUREEN. I don't know.

EDWARD. You didn't ask for their names?

MAUREEN. I didn't ask for their names why should I

EDWARD. Did it not cross your mind that I might have enemies?

MAUREEN. You're loved.

EDWARD. That over the years from time to time the children have heard about the history of the cane, sought to find evidence?

MAUREEN. They haven't.

EDWARD. Don't you understand that they came here hoping to find evidence? Tricking you into –?

MAUREEN. No. And they didn't anyway the ledger is safe.

EDWARD. The ledger yes but this I'm sure was a ruse to find

MAUREEN. What? To find? What?

EDWARD. Did it you give pleasure?

MAUREEN. I'm sorry.

EDWARD. Did it give you a thrill to let those kids in my attic? Did you gloat and cackle like an old witch?

MAUREEN. No!

EDWARD. To send unnamed children up into the attic, the attic that has always been mine, that I have organised and watched over, that was my space, for decades only for these –

ANNA. That's enough.

EDWARD. Have you no respect?

MAUREEN. For?

EDWARD. My authority.

MAUREEN. I apologise.

EDWARD. You silly bitch.

ANNA. That is not

EDWARD. You go. Up to the study. You work on the report while we

ANNA. No!

EDWARD. You don't want her interfering in our business do you?

MAUREEN. I don't

EDWARD. This is between me and my wife.

ANNA. I will not walk away when I see

EDWARD. Yes yes?

ANNA. Bullying.

EDWARD. I'm not bullying her. Am I bullying you? Answer me. Am I bullying you?

MAUREEN. No you're not bullying me.

EDWARD. There we go then there we go. That's clear. Go to your room.

ANNA. The bullied individual often doesn't identify themselves as the victim of

EDWARD. Victim?

ANNA. Yes victim.

EDWARD. It's always come round to that in the end doesn't it? Well maybe I'm the victim of

ANNA. No you're the

EDWARD. Too many bloody women. Give me that laptop. And the ledger. Hand it all over to me.

MAUREEN. Make up cuddle Daddy. Please.

EDWARD. I'm not in the

MAUREEN. Please please please please please please.

EDWARD. No.

MAUREEN. I was trying to make it special. To make Friday the most special wonderful

EDWARD. Friday won't go ahead.

MAUREEN. It has to

EDWARD. The Head won't show up this morning

MAUREEN. On his way.

EDWARD. No chance at all now that Friday will go ahead. Why do you do it eh?

MAUREEN. I don't mean to.

EDWARD. Why do you make me so angry?

ANNA. What's in the attic?

EDWARD. Work to be done.

ANNA. Is there something in the attic you didn't want

EDWARD. All forgotten now.

ANNA. Something you're worried that the kids could have discovered in the attic?

EDWARD. I'm very much a systems man. When I feel my systems have been disrupted then I have a tendency to overreact. Apologies to all concerned.

>   *(Bell rings.)*

MAUREEN. There we are I knew he'd come. The Head's a very loyal man. Do I look presentable?

EDWARD. You look more than presentable. You're as pretty as a peach.

ANNA. Are you sure that's the Head?

MAUREEN. Oh yes.

ANNA. That's a very insistent – he doesn't take his finger off the bell. Don't you think it's more likely to be the kids

MAUREEN. It's possible

ANNA. Coming to the door hoping to land a blow

MAUREEN. Do you

ANNA. Far more likely to be kids on the attack than the Head I'd say.

EDWARD. Let me

ANNA. I don't think that's a good

EDWARD. I'll deal with this.

ANNA. That will really provoke them.

EDWARD. I think this is better left to me.

>   *(Banging, shouting, the bell continues to ring.)*

It's time I stood up to them.

ANNA. No!

EDWARD. Hiding away. That's the coward's way. I'm going to stand up to the little buggers. Show them who's boss.

ANNA. If they have a brick

EDWARD. Let them throw whatever they've got.

ANNA. You mustn't open the door.

EDWARD. Are we going to spend our days hiding away? How long are we going to put up with this?

ANNA. Do you have pornography in the attic?

EDWARD. Please I

ANNA. It's understandable. Lots of men make use of pornography. I wouldn't judge.

EDWARD. I have never

ANNA. Most men in my experience somewhere have a stash

EDWARD. No

ANNA. I'd understand and I'm sure that she'd understand that if as a man you wanted to take yourself up into the attic and find some pleasure in

MAUREEN. Stop.

EDWARD. You have a sick mind.

ANNA. Or are the images maybe violent?

EDWARD. In the attic

ANNA. I can see that if the images are violent or if in some way they include images of children

MAUREEN. Stop that.

EDWARD. There's no pornography in the attic.

ANNA. None?

EDWARD. None not even the mildest there is nothing pornographic.

ANNA. Then why do you?

EDWARD. Because in the attic

ANNA. Yes?

EDWARD. In the attic is the cane.

TWO

(**EDWARD, MAUREEN, ANNA.**)

(A ladder.)

EDWARD. The cane for many years hung on the wall in the Deputy's office. It operated you see as much as a symbol as a – it was there as a warning. Beating was very much a last resort but as a threat. There it was. My first day in the job of Deputy Head. Hung on the wall as it had always hung. My instinct was of course to hide the cane away. A drawer, a cupboard. But I reasoned that that was actually more threatening. The children knowing that it was hidden was more frightening than it being there in plain sight for all to see. My first few weeks, it was somewhat disturbing to have the cane hanging there, watching over whatever I did. But you get used to things. The cane became part of the – almost I suppose part of the furniture. It was only when a child came into the office – you had to tell them "look at me, look into my eyes" – because their gaze would fall upon, they were transfixed by the cane. It was only when all the details were filled into the ledger – the child would be present when I filled in the details in the ledger – that I would finally remove the cane from the wall. And after the prescribed number of strokes had been given, I would return the cane immediately to the wall.

ANNA. Was there ever any blood?

EDWARD. Oh no.

ANNA. You never had to stop to wipe blood from the cane before returning it to the wall?

EDWARD. The cane doesn't break the surface of the skin.

ANNA. Not once?

EDWARD. You'd be doing something very wrong if you broke the surface of the skin.

ANNA. Were there welts?

EDWARD. I wouldn't say welts no.

ANNA. What would you?

EDWARD. There were marks. Red marks which in a day or so were gone.

ANNA. Ah well if it was only marks.

EDWARD. The whole thing was by and large a ritual.

ANNA. A very painful

EDWARD. Yes there was momentarily pain.

ANNA. A great deal of

EDWARD. Which many of the boys seemed to take a pride in. I'd watch them from my window and they would go directly from their caning and they'd go out into the playground and they would hold up the hand with the mark and the children would gather round them and they would cheer.

ANNA. Just because the victim

EDWARD. I suppose that's right

ANNA. Takes a perverted pride

EDWARD. I won't argue with you. When the legislation changed what should be done with the cane? There was no guidance. It was now illegal to cane a child but there were no instructions as to what to do with the cane. The government, the education authority, the governors, silent – the cane was suddenly to be erased from history. But how? There it was hanging on the wall. I removed it of course immediately, the day that the cane was outlawed, slid it behind my filing cabinet. Everyone who came in to my office – I could see their eyes go to the wall and they wanted to ask "Where did you put the cane?" But nobody asked because nobody now wanted to mention the cane at all. It remained behind the filing cabinet for I suppose a couple of years. But when it was announced that the next week my office was to be given a lick of paint, that over the weekend men would be coming to move the furniture out of my office – I was reminded of the cane's existence and I had to decide what to do with it.

MAUREEN. Destroy it.

EDWARD. Yes I suppose that would have been

MAUREEN. Break it into pieces and throw the pieces away.

EDWARD. Yes that would I suppose have been altogether the best option.

MAUREEN. Why didn't you?

EDWARD. Where I wonder did all the canes come from? Who supplied the canes to all the schools? Who were the manufacturers? Where did they source the wood? Did they have – hah! – catalogues and travelling salesmen?

MAUREEN. It would have been very easy to throw the cane away.

EDWARD. This cane is a very old cane. It was there when the school was a grammar and long before that – before even the railway, when all there was here were farms and a village school, the school master cut it I should imagine himself from a local tree. The cane is in my estimation a hundred-and-seventy-years old. It seemed to me disrespectful

ANNA. Disrespectful

EDWARD. Yes actually disrespectful to the generations of teachers and of boys, the cane which had left its mark on so many lives. I stood with it in my hands and the bin below – ready to break but I decided no.

MAUREEN. Why didn't you ask my permission?

EDWARD. Your permission?

MAUREEN. I think you should have asked my permission

EDWARD. We never discussed

MAUREEN. Before you brought the cane into our house?

EDWARD. When we had never once mentioned

MAUREEN. I would have told you that I didn't want it in our house.

EDWARD. We had neither of us had ever once mentioned the cane.

MAUREEN. When we both started

EDWARD. A long time ago.

MAUREEN. In teaching, we were agreed that we were against the cane.

EDWARD. Before yes.

ANNA. Is that right?

MAUREEN. We discussed, we voted at conference – yes, we wanted an end to the cane.

EDWARD. When we were student teachers yes, of course all the student teachers were yes. Opposed. There was blood actually. The very first time that I. There was of course no training as to how to cane a boy. My first boy was more experienced than I was. He was a naughty boy, the school's very naughtiest boy. A thief and in a small way an arsonist. He had been caned several times before by the previous Deputy Head so he knew how it worked but I – I misjudged the angle and the force of the blow. I broke the skin. A fleck of blood flew into my eye.

MAUREEN. We said that if we were ever in a position – we would refuse to give the cane.

EDWARD. For a woman, that was a theoretical

MAUREEN. It would be us who would end the practice of caning.

EDWARD. It was only the boys who were caned, it was only the male staff who did the caning. It was never a choice that any woman ever had to make. The boy looked at me with contempt to see what a fool I was to have actually broken the skin. He waited with disdain as I went for the first aid box, stuck a plaster over the broken skin. I'd denied him the welt to be displayed in the playground. After that as I became more practiced, I learnt to give just the right angle, the right force to leave a welt that was visible, livid but with no lasting damage done. If you hold the ladder.

MAUREEN. No.

EDWARD. I need you to hold the ladder.

MAUREEN. Why should I hold the ladder?

EDWARD. Because I want to go into the attic.

MAUREEN. Why do you want to go into the attic?

EDWARD. Because I want to know if the children you sent into the attic –

MAUREEN. You should be working on your report.

EDWARD. I want to know if they saw the cane.

MAUREEN. How will you know if they saw the cane?

EDWARD. When I was told that the furniture in my office would be moved, I wrapped the cane in a blanket and I carried it through the school and I put it in the boot of my car. For several months, it stayed there. But when I needed a new car, I then had to decide where to put the cane and the attic seemed like

MAUREEN. Tell him: the important thing is to finish his report.

EDWARD. I think on balance that the children in the attic must have unwrapped the blanket and seen the cane. That would explain why now the school has worked itself into a fury. I have to know if the blanket has been unwrapped.

MAUREEN. Wasting time in the attic when there's a report to be written.

EDWARD. Alright if you won't hold the ladder, then I shall just have to

MAUREEN. It will wobble.

EDWARD. That's the risk I'll take.

MAUREEN. And you will fall and break your neck.

EDWARD. Has it never crossed your mind that I exaggerated the risk of the wobble?

MAUREEN. Why would you do that?

EDWARD. That the possibility of falling and breaking my neck was almost entirely a fiction?

MAUREEN. I don't

EDWARD. Because I wanted you to feel that you had a part to play.

MAUREEN. Well then. Climb the ladder all by yourself.

EDWARD. Before we lived in a house with stairs and an attic, when we started at the school. We lived in a flat. I was very happy in the flat. The flat suited me very well.

MAUREEN. Let's not

EDWARD. But of course when you came along we needed all this.

MAUREEN. Go up into your attic.

EDWARD. I never wanted all this house.

MAUREEN. I think he's frightened to climb the ladder.

EDWARD. I had to pay for it all. Because once you came along, she was useless. Her hormones swung. She was depressed for years. And it was down to me to provide. Look about you. Everything here had to be paid for with what I earned. She used to cry when the bills came in. "How are we going to feed the baby?"

MAUREEN. If you're not going to use it then maybe you should put the ladder away?

EDWARD. So when I was offered Deputy, of course I had to take the job.

MAUREEN. You wanted

EDWARD. No actually

MAUREEN. You were very ambitious to be

EDWARD. Please don't tell me what I

MAUREEN. Up the greasy pole.

EDWARD. Everything had to be paid for and if that means putting the cane in the hand then alright yes put the cane in my hand and let the beating begin. You both lived very well because I

MAUREEN. Go up there and unwrap the blanket and look at your cane.

EDWARD. I will.

MAUREEN. And then bring your cane down here.

EDWARD. Maybe I'll

MAUREEN. Bring the cane down to me. And I'll destroy it. The ledger and the cane, torn and snapped away.

EDWARD. I suppose that's

MAUREEN. And let's never mention them ever again. Would you like me to hold the ladder?

EDWARD. For safety's sake

MAUREEN. For safety's sake it's better that I do yes?

EDWARD. Good firm grip.

MAUREEN. Up you go.

EDWARD. There's a wobble.

MAUREEN. No.

EDWARD. I felt a

MAUREEN. There's no wobble at all. You've imagined the wobble. Keep going.

EDWARD. It feels unsteady.

MAUREEN. You're almost there. Fetch the cane and bring the cane down here yes?

       (**EDWARD** *goes into the attic.*)

ANNA. Why do you think

MAUREEN. I don't know

ANNA. For all these years

MAUREEN. I have absolutely no idea

ANNA. He's kept the cane in the attic?

MAUREEN. Why don't you get on with the report?

ANNA. Did you have any idea? You never suspected

MAUREEN. Why would it cross my mind?

ANNA. That the cane was there?

MAUREEN. No.

ANNA. I thought maybe sending the children up there was your way of

MAUREEN. That's a very fanciful

ANNA. Maybe he kept the cane because

MAUREEN. The report has to be delivered first thing tomorrow.

ANNA. He thought that the pendulum would swing back.

MAUREEN. The window for a response to the inspectors closes tomorrow morning.

ANNA. They'd bring back the cane and he'd be ready

MAUREEN. It has to be finished tonight.

ANNA. Ready with the cane, to once again beat

MAUREEN. That's a very silly idea. Can you stop now please with all your silly ideas?

ANNA. The report is you know

MAUREEN. The inspectors invited the school to respond with a report.

ANNA. Of course yes the inspectors invite a response.

MAUREEN. The Head's such a weak man and so when your father offered

ANNA. But it is of course a formality.

MAUREEN. And he's been working tirelessly for weeks.

ANNA. The report won't change anything. You understand that?

MAUREEN. If you help him to get the wording right

ANNA. Once they've decided that a school is failing

MAUREEN. Will you take over the school?

ANNA. There is nothing that a report

MAUREEN. Will your academy add his school to its portfolio?

ANNA. Which of you decided that you wanted a child?

MAUREEN. It didn't work like that.

ANNA. Did either of you actually want a child?

MAUREEN. I'm sure we both wanted a child.

ANNA. That's what you

MAUREEN. It's the most natural thing in the world to want a child isn't it? You appreciate that as a mother of

ANNA. You discussed it together?

MAUREEN. I suppose I maybe yes I was the one who most wanted a child.

ANNA. And he?

MAUREEN. Well he

ANNA. Yes?

MAUREEN. Went along with it. He was more than happy to go along with it. I think that's often the way isn't it?

ANNA. I'm not sure that's

MAUREEN. The father of your children

ANNA. Was really quite useless. He took a lot of recreational pharmaceuticals.

MAUREEN. But you wanted the children so. He'd always be putting it off: tomorrow, tomorrow. So in the end, I just had to take the plunge, knowing that he'd go along with it when it happened. If I'd known of course about the depression that followed

ANNA. This coffee and these – what did you? – Portuguese tarts are I'm afraid an altogether wasted effort because it's very obvious that the Head isn't going to show up at all today. I have in my time, acted as a consultant to schools who need to write a response to an inspectors' report. We've both understood that it was all words. An invitation for a response has been made, a response must be written. None of the management of the school has the ability to write a response and they know anyway that it's a formality. The response will achieve nothing. But still the governors vote, the money is found and I'm brought in to write the document, which I do very well. The inspectors make a show of reading the report, it is duly noted and the school is passed over to the academy. This coffee is now you know quite cold. I made up all sorts of stories – little child, lying up there in my room, when it used to be my room – that I wasn't yours at all. You'd found me – washed up on the shore when you were on holiday in Bournemouth, I was left in the aisle of the Co-Op, a neighbour on her death bed passed me to you and you promised to bring me up as your own. You'll have quite a sum won't you once the endowment comes through from the mortgage and he gets his pension? You could travel. I can see you both on the Inca trail, that is I think something that you'd enjoy very much. And then you should get the work done on this house. Clear out the attic and go for a loft conversion. He's got his study why shouldn't you have a room? Do you have any hobbies? If you don't have one yet you should get one so that you can really make the most of the loft conversion. My children each have an instrument that they play but maybe an instrument is something that's best taken up in the earlier rather than in the last years of life?

(**ANNA** *empties the pot of coffee into the laptop.*)

Thomas plays the piano and Maddy plays the cello. At the moment it's a horrible noise but in time I'm hoping

MAUREEN. His work.

ANNA. We should have listened to you. Why didn't we listen to you? Never put coffee near a laptop.

MAUREEN. He wants to save the school.

ANNA. It's a waste of time.

MAUREEN. Are you sure of that?

ANNA. Empty words and now they're all gone.

MAUREEN. Are you going to hide?

ANNA. Am I going to hide what?

MAUREEN. Hide that.

ANNA. Why should I hide it?

MAUREEN. You hide it and I'll fetch a cloth to clean up the mess.

ANNA. Why would you do that?

MAUREEN. If he sees it

ANNA. Yes? What do you think he'll do if he sees it?

MAUREEN. I don't know. But I would imagine

ANNA. Yes?

MAUREEN. His rage is. I don't want more rage. Put it away, please.

EDWARD. I'm coming down now. Could somebody please hold the ladder?

MAUREEN. You'll take full responsibility for that.

EDWARD. Is there someone holding the ladder?

MAUREEN. Have you got the cane?

EDWARD. It was wrapped. The children – I'm sure – didn't see the cane.

MAUREEN. I'd like you to bring the cane down here please.

EDWARD. There's no need.

MAUREEN. Fetch the cane and bring it here.

EDWARD. Why would I do that?

MAUREEN. So that we can destroy the cane.

EDWARD. There's no need for that. Not today. Could somebody please hold the ladder?

MAUREEN. I'll only hold the ladder when you bring down the cane.

EDWARD. Why are you such a bloody difficult woman?

MAUREEN. Unless of course you're prepared to take the risk and break your neck.

EDWARD. Well, if you won't hold the ladder then I'm sure your daughter will. Come on sweetheart come and hold the ladder for your old dad.

ANNA. I think actually

EDWARD. Yes?

ANNA. I agree with Mum. Bring down the cane.

EDWARD. What's your game? I won't be told what to do in my house.

MAUREEN. Your house?

EDWARD. Bought and paid for. I can't – it's not stable. I can't unless one of you. If one of the coven won't – Please come on now don't be silly girls, enough is enough, playtime's over.

ANNA. Your grandchildren ask about you.

MAUREEN. Do they?

ANNA. All the time.

MAUREEN. What do you tell them about us?

ANNA. I tell them that you're both very lovely.

MAUREEN. That's nice.

ANNA. Very kind. Devoted to each other. They want to see you.

MAUREEN. I suppose

ANNA. And you know anytime you want me to drive you to the cottage, it's only forty-five minutes. I have a spare room. You're welcome to stay for as long as you want.

MAUREEN. I'd like that.

ANNA. Thomas will play his piano, Maddy will play the cello. Please be indulgent. It's not a pleasant noise but in time

MAUREEN. Of course.

ANNA. Maybe they'll show you one of their stories. They make up little stories about you and him, with their glove puppets.

MAUREEN. Really?

ANNA. Sometimes it's a little bit Punch and Judy but on the whole they're very funny stories.

EDWARD. What are you saying down there?

ANNA. We're just gossipping isn't that right?

MAUREEN. That's right just having a good old gossip. Girls.

EDWARD. Well could you girls stop gossiping and hold the ladder?

ANNA. I'll hold the ladder.

EDWARD. Thank you.

ANNA. When you bring down the cane.

MAUREEN. It's a shame not to put that card up isn't it?

ANNA. I think so.

MAUREEN. After the children made all the effort. Here give it to me and I'll

ANNA. They'll be delighted to know it's found a home.

MAUREEN. It looks lovely there. It really brightens the place up.

ANNA. It's mostly stickers. They're not the most imaginative

MAUREEN. I think it's beautiful.

EDWARD. Orders obeyed. I've got the cane.

ANNA. I'm holding the ladder.

EDWARD. It needs a good firm grip.

ANNA. I know that.

EDWARD. I don't want to break my neck do I?

ANNA. I don't think any of us want you to break your neck. How about if I put my foot on the bottom rung? Does that feel better with my foot on the bottom rung?

EDWARD. Yes, that's better.

ANNA. I thought that would make the difference.

MAUREEN. Is that the cane?

> *(Noises off.)*

Listen to that.

EDWARD. What's that?

MAUREEN. They suddenly got louder. I'd say that's the loudest they'd ever been wouldn't you?

EDWARD. I don't know.

MAUREEN. I didn't have noise-blocking headphones for the last six days I've been listening and listening and that is definitely the loudest.

EDWARD. Who put up that card?

MAUREEN. That's by far the loudest they've ever been.

EDWARD. It's not the place that I'd have chosen for the card but

MAUREEN. How many children do you think there are out there now?

EDWARD. It actually looks quite nice there.

MAUREEN. If you had to calculate how many children do you think are outside that door now?

EDWARD. Well I suppose there must be I would say close to two hundred.

MAUREEN. Why are there more than ever?

EDWARD. You think

MAUREEN. It seems

EDWARD. That they know that the cane is here?

MAUREEN. I don't see how

EDWARD. Exactly there's no way that they could know that the cane is here. You mustn't let your imagination. You've lived for several decades with the cane directly above the bed where you slept and you never

MAUREEN. I don't think so.

EDWARD. You don't think so?

MAUREEN. I suppose sometimes a feeling that something wasn't quite

EDWARD. A feeling isn't

MAUREEN. No you're right a general feeling isn't

EDWARD. So there's no possible reason that the children know that the cane is here.

ANNA. Are you going to unwrap it?

EDWARD. I thought we could

ANNA. I think you should unwrap it.

EDWARD. I'd rather dispose of it as it is.

ANNA. Why's that?

EDWARD. I suppose because I don't feel very much like looking at it.

ANNA. You haven't looked at in all these years?

EDWARD. That's right.

ANNA. I'd imagined

EDWARD. Yes?

ANNA. From time to time, that you'd gone up into the attic and that'd you'd unwrapped

EDWARD. No

ANNA. the blanket and taken a look at the cane.

EDWARD. Never. Why would I?

ANNA. Why would you look at the cane?

EDWARD. Yes why would I look at the cane?

ANNA. I don't know maybe for old time's sake.

EDWARD. You're right. It should be destroyed.

ANNA. And maybe even that you'd taken the cane out of the blanket and that for old times sake you'd swished it about?

EDWARD. Swished it about?

ANNA. For the sense of power.

EDWARD. Good Lord, no. Once it's dark and the mob has dispersed, we'll build a bonfire and we'll burn the bundle and the ledger. That's the best thing to do.

ANNA. Have you ever seen the cane?

MAUREEN. Never.

ANNA. Would you like to see the cane?

EDWARD. I'm going to leave it here until it's dark. The most important thing is to finish the report.

MAUREEN. I would actually like to see the cane.

EDWARD. Why's that?

MAUREEN. I suppose because I'm curious.

EDWARD. It's only a cane.

MAUREEN. I would sometimes you know I'd be making your breakfast and I'd wonder is he going to be called upon to cane a boy today? Or at the supermarket: I wonder if right now there's a boy with his hand held out and the cane is being beaten into his palm? Or getting into the bed with you at night: perhaps this is a man who has today caned.

EDWARD. You thought that?

MAUREEN. Not so very often. Most of the time, not all. But occasionally. Should I have told you?

EDWARD. No.

MAUREEN. That's what I thought.

ANNA. Shall we pick up where we left off at pupil voice? I think if we make one last push on pupil voice.

MAUREEN. I'll unwrap it myself.

EDWARD. No.

MAUREEN. If you're not going to.

EDWARD. Alright then have it your own way. You always do.

(**MAUREEN** *unwraps the cane.)*

MAUREEN. Is that it?

EDWARD. Yes that's it. What were you expecting?

MAUREEN. I suppose something altogether

EDWARD. Yes?

MAUREEN. Bigger.

EDWARD. Ah well.

MAUREEN. It seems very small to me. Does it seem small to you?

ANNA. Yes I suppose it does.

MAUREEN. In my head it was a great big but actually. What did you imagine?

EDWARD. It's not a cudgel. Or a club.

MAUREEN. Even so.

EDWARD. The aim is not to smash the brains out of an opponent but to deliver a swift, sharp stroke. A number of swift, sharp strokes. Appropriate to the misdemeanour. According to the rules set down.

MAUREEN. It's actually really rather puny.

EDWARD. I suppose when it was first fashioned everyone was very much smaller. Both teacher and child. Everyone in the past was shorter. Without the nutrition. Even thirty years ago, the children were by and large scrawny. The children now are great big, tall, fat. And to the child at the time – you've got to imagine from a child's perspective at the time it wasn't so tiny.

MAUREEN. Did a cane never snap?

EDWARD. Never.

MAUREEN. I would have thought such a puny

EDWARD. The strength lies in the flexibility.

MAUREEN. But even so it must be very easy to break

EDWARD. It's a lot stronger than it looks.

MAUREEN. Take this firmly in both hands and pull and you could snap it in two.

EDWARD. No actually no.

MAUREEN. How do you know? Have you tried? Do it now. Take it and snap it in two.

EDWARD. I'm not going to do that.

MAUREEN. Why not? Why wait for tonight when you can do it

EDWARD. No! I've said no and I mean no. You have to learn to listen to me when I say no. You make yourself busy in the kitchen while me and her

ANNA. You know that the Head isn't coming?

EDWARD. I can see that yes.

ANNA. Why do you think that the Head isn't coming?

EDWARD. Because he's not a strong man.

ANNA. No?

EDWARD. Because he's a weak man. So I suppose if the governors have got to him

ANNA. They'll be following best practice.

EDWARD. Then he'll be obeying their orders.

ANNA. What do you think they will have advised him?

EDWARD. They will have advised him that it's best if Friday doesn't go ahead. Would you say they would advise that was best?

ANNA. Yes, I would say that yes they would have advised him that Friday shouldn't go ahead.

EDWARD. Ah well.

ANNA. I would say that under the current circumstances you won't be given a leaving do on Friday.

EDWARD. That was I suppose

ANNA. Yes?

EDWARD. A vanity. It's really not necessary to have all the children parading around the hall, dressed up as me, singing songs, that's all – I suppose in practice that might be somewhat embarrassing and even – ha – undignified mightn't it? I didn't give forty-five years so that I could be presented with a pageant. That is I can see now totally unnecessary. A couple of drinks in several months' time with a few colleagues. That if I'm honest would suit me altogether better. Or maybe once this is all redecorated, nice summer day, we can have a few of them here for a barbecue – bangers and beer – what do you think?

MAUREEN. I suppose that might

EDWARD. Once the endowment comes through, the pension and decorate

MAUREEN. Yes, we'll get some men in

EDWARD. I thought I'd

MAUREEN. No no we'll employ

EDWARD. I'll need something to fill up my time

MAUREEN. Someone to do the job properly.

EDWARD. Properly? I'll do the job properly.

MAUREEN. No you won't. You know you won't. You'll talk and talk about it, you'll make plans but you'll never actually

EDWARD. How can you say?

MAUREEN. But you'll never actually do it. If you want people here in a few months' time for a barbecue in a freshly decorated house then we'll get some men in to

EDWARD. If you think that's best.

MAUREEN. I do.

EDWARD. Then we'll

MAUREEN. And I thought also we could have the attic cleared and have a loft conversion.

EDWARD. Why do you want a loft conversion?

MAUREEN. It's a waste. An attic full of junk.

EDWARD. Mementoes.

MAUREEN. We could have an extra room.

EDWARD. We don't need an extra room.

MAUREEN. I'd like an extra room.

EDWARD. Would you?

MAUREEN. Yes for my study.

EDWARD. Your study? What will you study in your study?

MAUREEN. I don't know.

EDWARD. You've never shown any interest in studying.

MAUREEN. I might take up an instrument.

EDWARD. Really?

MAUREEN. Perhaps the cello.

EDWARD. The cello? That would make a terrible racket.

MAUREEN. With a really good loft conversion you wouldn't hear a thing. And there's always your noise-blocking headphones isn't there?

EDWARD. You've got it all worked out.

MAUREEN. Would you like me to bring you your headphones now so that you can continue with the report?

EDWARD. I didn't actually find the headphones all that

MAUREEN. Well then.

EDWARD. The headphones didn't suit me. I gave them a good try but I actually found them irritating.

MAUREEN. Irritating?

EDWARD. Yes they irritated my ears.

MAUREEN. So they were an altogether wasted birthday present?

EDWARD. Children making noise – forty-five years in school – is something I'm very much used to. I gave up on the headphones after the first few hours and I pressed on with my work. A hundred children shouting outside the window wasn't going to distract me from saving the school. I should I can see have tried earlier to understand pupil voice. Over the years I suppose one becomes suspicious – there's always fresh jargon – but if I'd understood and implemented pupil voice. Perhaps I should have asked for your advice a little sooner?

ANNA. I think perhaps you should.

EDWARD. But at least there's enough time before the deadline to get to work on – Oh. What's happened to the laptop? Someone's switched off the – who switched off the? Come on. Somebody must have switched off the. I hoped you saved. Oh. I can't get it to. Am I doing this right? The laptop is. Oh. Wet. Fluid has penetrated the. Ah. The laptop is dead. My report is lost. Six days' work to save the school has been destroyed. Someone has it seems spilled – who was responsible for spilling coffee – a considerable amount of coffee over my laptop? Did you spill coffee over my laptop?

ANNA. It was me.

EDWARD. How could you have been so careless?

ANNA. I wasn't careless.

EDWARD. I would call it incredibly careless to place the coffee pot so close to the laptop.

ANNA. It didn't happen because of carelessness.

EDWARD. And then so clumsily knock

ANNA. It was done with great care. I very carefully poured the coffee

EDWARD. Why would you?

ANNA. into the laptop.

EDWARD. Why?

ANNA. To destroy the laptop. To destroy your work.

EDWARD. I see. The laptop isn't my property. The laptop is school property. I was lent the laptop so that I could work from home, write the report to the inspectors. Tomorrow I have to return the laptop. How can I explain to the Head?

ANNA. The report was useless.

EDWARD. You understand that you have damaged school property?

ANNA. I understand.

EDWARD. How can I now save the school?

ANNA. The report was a waste of time so I washed it away with coffee.

EDWARD. Silly little bitch. Cunt.

ANNA. What I wonder nowadays is the appropriate punishment for damaging school property? Now that you've been denied the cane what's the

EDWARD. I should have nipped this in the bud. When you – all those years ago – destroyed this room

ANNA. Bring out the belt?

EDWARD. No.

ANNA. Give the kid a good whack like your dear old Dad?

EDWARD. I should have been less tolerant.

ANNA. All of our academy schools operate an eyes forward policy. Students must keep their eyes to the front of the class at all times. At all times, staff must be able to see into student's eyes. The student must seek permission if at any time they want to turn their head or turn their back upon a teacher. Permission is of course never unreasonably withheld. It's difficult often for students whose school has only recently acquired academy status. Where before there has been only chaos the transition to order can be very challenging. But after a few weeks – I've seen it happen time and time again – eyes forward becomes second nature and a great calmness falls upon the child and spreads through the school.

EDWARD. Acquiescence.

ANNA. We also have a silence policy. Nobody speaks in the classroom unless they're invited by the teacher. The corridors are entirely silent spaces. Eyes forward, lips sealed and move to the next class. Pupils report that formerly they found the move from room to room a frightening, threatening time but now they enjoy the calm. Listen to those young people out there. Their anger. Is their anger about the cane? About you? What do you think?

EDWARD. I would say

ANNA. I would say no. You've become a focus for a wider sense of

EDWARD. Will your academy?

ANNA. There's a much wider chaos.

EDWARD. Will you be seeking to introduce your eyes forward policy into my school?

ANNA. Your school? Time you let go.

EDWARD. Will next year my students be moving silently through the corridors?

ANNA. After Friday, you can concentrate on decorating, travelling. Anytime you want to visit your grandchildren. They ask for you. It's been indicated to me – yes – that any proposal we make as an academy for management of the school now it's been identified as failing will be given serious consideration.

EDWARD. Look what you gave birth to.

MAUREEN. I asked and she promised.

EDWARD. The snake's crawling out of the grass.

MAUREEN. You promised me that you wouldn't take his school.

ANNA. We will only make a bid if I consider it's in the best interest of the students

EDWARD. Poison.

ANNA. To make the transition to an academy. Don't you think I should be punished?

MAUREEN. Stop that.

ANNA. Damage to school property. That surely

MAUREEN. There's no point

ANNA. Shouldn't go unpunished?

MAUREEN. Making him angry.

ANNA. Let's get out the ledger. And a pen. Let's start the process. Here I'm writing my name in the book.

MAUREEN. Don't be a silly girl.

ANNA. And I'm writing my crime. Damage to school property.

MAUREEN. Apologise to him.

ANNA. What – according to the guidelines – are the appropriate number of strokes for damage to school property?

MAUREEN. If you ask properly

ANNA. I see here, that a similar case received five

MAUREEN. Find the right words and he'll forgive you.

ANNA. Should let's say five. Five strokes of the cane to my hand.

MAUREEN. Silly silly girl.

ANNA. Now then parental permission. Which of you will give permission for five strokes of the cane to the hand for the damage of school property? Does one of you need to give permission or as a parent myself can I? I'll sign it myself. My own parent. There we are. Parental permission given. It's all done. Five strokes of the cane to the hand. I'm ready.

EDWARD. Your hand is shaking.

ANNA. No.

EDWARD. Your hand is – there's a considerable shake.

ANNA. Is that right?

EDWARD. A hand like that can't be caned. Only a firm hand can receive the cane.

ANNA. The boys' hands never shook?

EDWARD. I don't remember.

ANNA. I find it hard to believe that no boy ever

EDWARD. I suppose they must have done only I can't

ANNA. What do you think you would have done if the boy's hand shook?

EDWARD. I suppose

ANNA. Would the boy be excused the cane?

EDWARD. I don't think so.

ANNA. That would hardly be effective would it? Shake your hand and you're excused the cane?

EDWARD. We wouldn't have done it like that.

ANNA. You would have proceeded with the caning?

EDWARD. Yes.

ANNA. So what would you?

EDWARD. I suppose I would have spoken softly and calmly to the boy, I would have reassured the boy that there would be pain but the pain would pass and it was there for reasons of justice and learning.

ANNA. You remember doing that?

EDWARD. I don't remember that but I suppose.

ANNA. What would you say?

EDWARD. I'd say: "You understood didn't you what the rules were? The rules were very clear and yet you chose to break the rules. And in breaking the rules you knew what your punishment would be. And now is the time to take your punishment and after that there will be time to reflect and to ask yourself: Will I ever break the rules again? What I'm about to do to you isn't personal. It's not that I want revenge or that I'm angry with you. It's not that I dislike you or that I think that you're a sinner. You're simply a boy who has broken the rules and I'm simply someone who is enforcing the rules and I will do this simply and efficiently, without cruelty, without pleasure. Is that clear to you?'

ANNA. And if reassuring words didn't work?

EDWARD. I don't remember any instance when

ANNA. What do you imagine you would do?

EDWARD. I suppose I would support the boy's hand until the shaking had passed.

ANNA. Like this.

EDWARD. Yes.

ANNA. You'd hold the hand for as long as it took for the shaking to pass.

EDWARD. That's right.

ANNA. And then you'd take the cane from the wall?

EDWARD. No I imagine that I would have already taken the cane from the wall.

ANNA. Yes?

EDWARD. I would already have taken the cane from the wall and I would have placed the cane on the desk.

ANNA. So that once the hand was still you could move directly to the

EDWARD. Exactly.

MAUREEN. It looks so puny but it won't I try and I try but it won't snap.

ANNA. My hand's still now.

EDWARD. Are you sure?

ANNA. Take your hand away and you'll – see? The shaking's gone. Five lashes.

MAUREEN. Why won't it snap? There's got to be a way to make it snap.

EDWARD. It was a matter of pride for all the boys I think that their faces never gave anything anyway. I was always on the watch for the trembling lip, little tear. Perhaps a flash of anger in their eyes. But as far as I can recall there was never any of that. Always the same expression. Dead.

(**EDWARD** *canes* **ANNA** *once.*)

One. That's what I always do you see? I think it's fairer you see to count aloud. So that the boy knows what to expect. And to judge the gap between – too long prolongs the experience but too quickly – you see?

MAUREEN. You've broken the skin.

EDWARD. Have I?

MAUREEN. See what you've done. There's blood.

EDWARD. Ah yes.

MAUREEN. A welt and it's pouring blood.

EDWARD. I must I suppose be out of practice.

ANNA. If you leave it too long

EDWARD. Any man after all this time would be out of practice wouldn't they?

ANNA. It's worse if you leave it too long.

EDWARD. You forget: the correct angle, the correct force of the blow.

ANNA. You need to move on: number two.

EDWARD. I can't when there's a welt.

ANNA. The rules say five blows.

EDWARD. Not when I've broken the skin.

MAUREEN. That's it. Stop now. Everything done and we'll dress the wound.

ANNA. It doesn't need no. The boy whose wound was dressed had nothing to show the crowd. And I've got to have something to show the crowd.

MAUREEN. We have a first aid box. Everything we need is in the first aid box. Somewhere there's a first aid box. Where do we keep the first aid box? There's a special place where we keep the first aid box. I should know at all times where to locate the first aid box. Because really what is the point of a first aid box if it can't be located in an emergency? I suppose at one time I must have known where the first aid box was but now I can't remember. Sometimes if you close your eyes and picture the last time and you... Nothing. Nothing. Where do you suppose the first aid box can be? Do you think maybe on one of your expeditions up into the attic that you've taken the first aid box with you and then you've forgotten that you've taken it up there and forgetting that you've taken it up there, you've left it there? Would you say the attic is a likely place to locate the first aid box? We've really been very lucky haven't we? Who can say that years and years have gone by without so much as a cut finger or a grazed knee? I think actually the last time there was blood in this house was when she broke the mirror and you cut your finger picking up the shards. And that must have been a long, long time ago because she was no higher than. I think really the only place that the first aid box can be is in the attic. Why don't I go up into the attic and bring down the first aid box and then we can see to that wound? Only I can't go up unless someone holds the ladder. I'd be too frightened of falling and breaking me neck if there isn't somebody at the bottom steadying the ladder. Come on somebody. One of you. Somebody hold the ladder.

ANNA. I'm going outside now.

EDWARD. Yes?

ANNA. I'm going to raise my hand like this.

EDWARD. I see.

ANNA. Display the welt and the blood to the mob.

EDWARD. Of course.

ANNA. What do you think they'll do when they see the welt? Two hundred children? When I tell them that you've kept the cane here all these years? And that you've caned me here today?

EDWARD. They'll be angry.

ANNA. They will. So angry that they'll force their way in here. They'll see the ledger and the cane. And if they look in the cupboard under the stairs they'll find the axe. And if they find the axe they'll hold you down and chop off your head and carry your head from the house to the school and spit on it as it passes by.

EDWARD. Tell them: There's hundreds of men. Tell them: they'll be in their sixties now, seventies, eighties. Tell them: if a man was a Head or a Deputy Head of a school, then the chances are that they gave the cane. Tell them: those men are too proud to ask for your forgiveness. Tell them: those men would be insulted – yes insulted and diminished by your forgiveness. Tell them: if you check the records, you'll be able to locate those men. And if the records have been lost or destroyed tell them to ask every man over sixty who has been a Head or a Deputy Head: How many boys did you cane? Tell them: On the whole these men aren't liars and they'll tell you honestly – as best as their memory allows – how many boys they've caned. Tell them: if you feel it's necessary, set up tribunals, the school hall, the town hall, television or web cam. And bring those men – force them from their villas in Spain or their retirement homes, force them from the garden centres and the local history groups – and stand them before the tribunals. And let all the fat bald men who were once boys who were caned accuse those men and let the caned decide what the punishment for those old men should be. And do it soon before all of us old men lose our memories and escape to our graves.

(**ANNA** *leaves.*)

End

Milton Keynes UK
Ingram Content Group UK Ltd.
UKHW050412030824
446490UK00009B/341